COLORING TIGER

G000293441

Coloring Books for Adults Relaxation

MY BOSS IS A JERK

MARK THOMPSON

COLORING BOOKS FOR ADULTS
RELAXATION: MY BOSS IS A JERK

Published in 2018 by Coloring Tiger

Email: mark@coloringtiger.com
Website: www.coloringtiger.com

ISBN-13: 978-0-9996722-5-9

COLORING TIGER™
Art for Creative Expression

THIS BOOK BELONGS TO

_____

_____

COLOR TEST PAGE

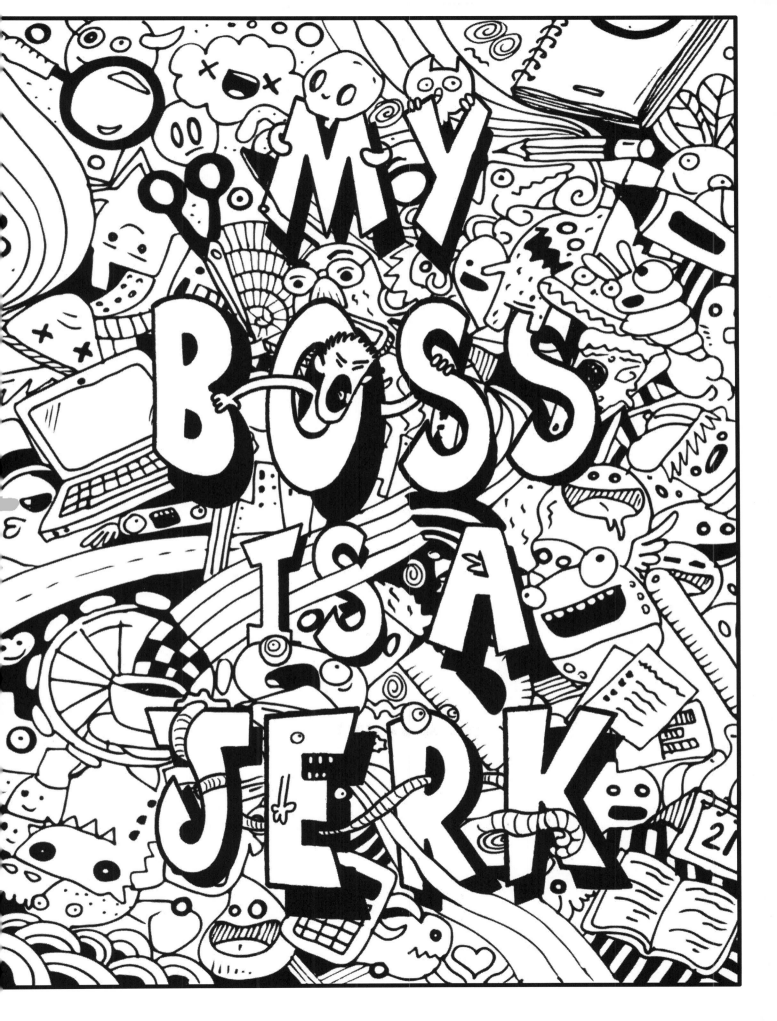

Printed in Great Britain
by Amazon